KT-197-662

On Happiness

On Happiness

ROY STRONG

LONG BARN BOOKS

PUBLISHED BY
LONG BARN BOOKS

Ebrington, Gloucestershire GL55 6NW

First published in 1997
1 3 5 7 9 10 8 6 4 2

Set in 11/16pt Monotype Bembo
Printed and bound by Redwood Books, Trowbridge, Wiltshire

ISBN 0 952 8285 4 5

Preface

This essay was delivered as the Nineteenth Baggs Memorial Lecture at the University of Birmingham on Tuesday 19 November 1996. The subject of this lecture is immoveable, Happiness, and, having tackled it, I can well understand why one lecturer withdrew a week before it had to be delivered. It is a demanding but, I found, in the end, a rewarding topic. In printing it I am able to recall what proved to be a happy occasion. Putting it into book form has also given yet another opportunity for happiness, collaboration with my wife, who has provided the delightful accompanying drawings.

I am more than grateful to Susan Hill and

Long Barn Books for including this among their publications.

ROY STRONG

The Laskett, Autumn 1977

WILLIAM
LARKIN
ESQ.

My eyelids generally open each morning at a few minutes before seven. By then, even in winter, enough light is filtering into the bedroom for me to make out some of the objects which cover its walls, for this is a house of shared memory.

Against the pale green wallpaper, a small water-colour, of a table laid for two in a Herefordshire cider apple orchard, catches my eye. It was the gift of a friend, the painter John Ward, who taught my wife to draw and I know he would have put that table in his picture with us in mind, sitting beneath the rosy fruit.

Over to the left, on the window wall, is a portrait

of one of our most beloved cats, the Rev. Wenceslas Muff (a curious name I am aware but, as T. S. Eliot wrote, you must never give a cat a dull name.) He was called Muff because he looked like a lady's fur muff, Wenceslas because he resembled the seventeenth-century Czech artist Wenceslas Hollar's engraving of one, and a cleric because he was black. Now he rests beneath the earth in the garden, with a monument above topped by a golden ball, catching the sunlight. Many tears were shed on that day.

Against the wall opposite the bed an old trunk festooned with cushions acts as a resting place for a growing family of teddy bears, the oldest, Pluto, now with one eye, was born in the same year as my wife – 1930 – the youngest a pair which we gave each other recently as we sailed to New York on the QE2.

I could continue. But, as you see, the day begins with happiness of the kind which memory brings. When we are dead and gone these things, a melange

of pictures and objects, will have lost their context and their meaning. To those that come after they will just be a few old soft toys, a pretty watercolour and a painting of a cat. To me, each single thing recalls a moment of the shared happiness of marriage, one which is built upon the richness of association, in terms of time and place, of often quite mundane things which radiate resonances only to the two people concerned. Even when only one of the pair is left that triggering of the mind and emotions will remain.

I put on my dressing gown, go down the stairs and swing wide the door into the kitchen. There, every morning, I am greeted by a sight which always fills me with delight. On the kitchen counter opposite the Aga a multi-coloured duvet is spread and on it, either still asleep or just bestirring themselves, are our two cats, Larkin and Souci – shortened versions of their full names: William Larkin Esquire of The Laskett, named not after the poet but after an obscure Jacobean painter, and Herzog Friedrich von Sans Souci, the result of a visit to Potsdam. Both are American Maine Coons, monster long-haired creatures with tails like nodding ostrich plumes, huge ears and vast eyes which survey you as though receiving radar signals. They are half-brothers, thanks

HERZOG
FREDERICK
VON SANS
SOUCI

to interbreeding in a manner not in accordance with the consanguinity rules of the Church of England. They are also strongly contrasted in character. Larkin, a silver tabby, was born, like John Betjeman, to be a geriatric, timid, a trifle reclusive, hiding his need for affection most of the time, and with tendencies to melancholia. Souci, tabby and white, hasn't a care in the world, fully living up to his name, Sans Souci, trotting around all day squeaking or rolling over in glee and waving his long white legs in the air. He is, in short, a happy cat.

I have dwelt on that early morning encounter in which I press my nose into their warm fur with pleasure and listen to the purrs, because their innate dispositions reflect exactly what I have read about research into happiness. Here we have two domestic pets, one from birth a happy soul who rebounds easily from reverses, the other with a tendency to tilt downwards. On my writing-room shelf is a box file labelled 'Happiness' in which I have been storing every newspaper article I came across on the subject – and it is surprising just how much happiness, as an achievable state, has preoccupied the media. Reading through the cuttings, I found that there emerged one generally agreed scientific consensus; that happiness, which everyone defined as 'subjective well-being' is in part heritable. In studying this phenomenon much use was made of twins, and it was discovered that those with the same genes invariably had a happiness score which was correlated.

Out of all this material it emerged that there are three identifiable groups. Into the first fall those who have the good fortune to be born happy and who pick up easily from reverses, others for whom a reverse only topples them downwards, and finally a mid-way group who, if aware of the latter inclination, can by a exercise of will pull themselves out of it. So happiness may, for many, be chosen, and that surely is something for which to be grateful.

Aristotle defined happiness as the goal of all human activity and ever since, poets and philosophers have pondered on it. Today it is the turn of psychiatrists, psychologists and psychotherapists who battle with the evolving science of brain chemistry. All of that is quite beyond me but, taking into account that happiness is in part heritable, I give you what Michael Argyle, Emeritus Professor of Social Psychology at Wolfson College, Oxford identifies as its component parts. These are: positive emotions like joy, the absence of negative ones like anxiety, and a non-emotional component which amounts to a general feeling of contentment or satisfaction with your life. And, hardly surprisingly, a loving relationship is by far the greatest source of contentment. Well, I'd go along with that. Happiness was only loosely linked to wealth, the unemployed emerging as only marginally less happy than the rich – in other words it doesn't come with winning the lottery. Then there are the experiments, in one of which people were asked to respond by placing themselves on a 'satisfaction with life' scale, in another they were asked to record their mood every time a bleeper went off. The result of this survey, taken in the 1980s, was that, in terms of the happiness barometer, the Japanese and Germans scored in the sixes, the Americans in the sevens and the British 7.5. Is this, I wondered, evidence of island euphoria?

Perhaps it only goes to confirm Archbishop Richard Whateley's witty remark that 'Happiness is no laughing matter,' – although when it comes to Happiness quotations I have a certain sympathy with Dr Johnson's observation that 'There is nothing which has yet been contrived by man, by which so much happiness is produced as by a good tavern or inn.' None of this scientific claptrap seems to get me much further than the conclusion that on the whole I am a happy person, probably falling into the first category of the three, and it only confirms my belief that any account of happiness must be a subjective one.

To be aware of happiness, even if that state is registered only in retrospect, you must have experienced unhappiness. As I get older, I keep pondering whether it is in the accident of birth and childhood or in the uncertainties of old age that most of life's cruellest and least predictable miseries lie. I wish I could say that I had a happy childhood, but I did not, just how unhappy was not registered at the time; that could only happen by looking back from what seem the golden days of later life. As a child you are unaware of any circumstance other than the one into which you have been born. I was certainly never ill-treated or abused and it was no fault of my parents that the Second World War broke out when I was four. Even by then their marriage was a fractured one and I grew up in a divided household, sharpened by the physical confines of a 1920s North London suburban terrace house. Inevitably one recalls Philip Larkin's famously blunt line about parents 'They fuck you up, your Mum and Dad' or Oscar Wilde's more quotable one, 'When you grow up you judge your parents. Sometimes you forgive them.'

What can be seen in retrospect is that unhappiness begets growth, or a least it did in my case. I retreated from the malign atmosphere of an unhappy household and the deprivations of war by creating an imaginary world, either by sitting painting or by playing with toy theatres, or studying. In each instance it was a retreat into the past, for the pictures only ever figured people in period costume, the plays were the nineteenth century melodramas which came with Pollock's toy theatre and the books I read were history. Happiness was achievable through an exercise of the intellect and the imagination in order to live in the past. I can see now how it must have fuelled my passion for history and then for museums, for both were escapes from an unhappy present. Is one allowed to give thanks for unhappiness? That seems a strange thing to do, but from the plateau of my seventh decade, when one is on, as it were, the homeward stretch, I think that one can, for it was those particular personal circumstances that provided me with much of my life's work.

They also presented me with an environment from which I needed to escape. It was not until my middle twenties, when at long last I managed to make an exit from suburbia and the family that I was to discover the joys and excitement of the present. All the same, thanks to having passed twenty five years of my life in what was in many ways an inimical atmosphere, I have never lost that ability to switch off from the now and disappear into the past.

That has seen me through innumerable crises. Even in my darkest hours as Director of the Victoria & Albert Museum, beleaguered by rabid trades unions, hostile media and intractable trustees, I was able to go into my writing room and within minutes be living in another age. That is truly a form of happiness for which to be grateful, for all it demands is a flat surface, some paper, a pen and books. It is self-contained, dependent on no one else except oneself, for it is all self-generated. Those who write have a rare privilege – that of living more than one life. From my middle twenties I have never been without a book in the pipeline. Some have been better than others, some have been more enjoyable than others to research and write, but collectively they embody not only a sense of achievement but a form of happiness reached through the exercise of the creative intellect. In those moods of depression which can strike occasionally I suddenly throw open the glass doors of the bookcase in which the collected works are housed and pull the odd book down and turn its pages, just to cheer myself up.

Childhood was not the only unhappy period of my life, though it was certainly the loneliest and the longest. But that was unhappiness. This essay is about the opposite. For every single person, happiness means something slightly different, whether it is a distant memory or something firmly rooted in present reality. Whatever those happy things are they form a garland decked across the mind whose blossoms see one through the dark days.

Over the years I have kept a patchy diary, and recently, I have been editing those years which cover my public career, between 1967 and 1987 – from the ages of thirty two to fifty-two – first as Director of the National Portrait Gallery and then of the Victoria & Albert Museum. The story they tell has been enlarged by a series of letters I wrote to a Dutch academic friend. Initially I had set aside a year for this task but I found that reliving my own past was so disturbing that I virtually sat immovable at the computer screen until I had finished all six hundred pages in just three months. Much of it was deeply unhappy, and that was what made the task such a traumatic one, but going through it all after the event I was also struck by how often it was that I actually wrote of happiness and how certain things which embodied it saw me through.

The first of these was marriage. 'Now I can tell you,' I wrote to Jan van Dorsten on 9 September 1971, 'as by the time this reaches you it will have happened. I will have eloped and married Julia Trevelyan Oman. Unbeknown to everyone, to parents specially, I asked Julia to marry me on 21 July. I can't tell you how thrilled and happy I am about it all.' Eight years later I was to write to him: 'Next Monday we will have been married eight years and my only regret is that it was not longer.' The letter continues in the light of the knowledge that he was about to marry for the third time: 'we wish you both all the loving happiness we have had and have every-day, all the eating together, the cooking, the washing up, the planting and weeding, the working, the everything – it is the most precious thing ever given.' A month later follows a reflective piece dwelling on having reached what almost twenty years on seems the positively young age of forty four. But it was written five years into what proved to be a tempes-tuous reign at the Victoria & Albert Museum coping with government cuts and militant unions.

'I am forty four this year,' it begins, 'It is quite difficult to even think what lies ahead because it seems so much a period which might be categorized as the years between: I am neither the brash young swinging sixties museum director, nor the doyen of the art establishment. On the whole one is content. Privately I have been blessed with abundant happiness with Julia and our life together. That has been the most precious and miraculous gift of all, stabilizing and consoling through every crisis. Our house, The Laskett, my writing room, the garden and its changing seasons give me perpetual joy.'

In that paragraph, written during a period of deep public unhappiness when at times it seemed that all I had striven for lay in ruins around me, I listed off those things that brought the blessed counterpoint of happiness, although it did not include – but should have done – a cat, our first, the Lady Torte de Shell, for by then she had climbed up the wisteria to our bedroom window and gone to sleep on my head as a sign that she wished to stay, which indeed she did and was greatly beloved.

But what of that house, that writing room and that garden? What kind of happiness do they embody? The house is a red sandstone one on the

Welsh Borders, which we purchased in 1972, a year after we married. Everyone knows that magic moment when they alight on what they believe will be their future home – or at least I hope they do, for the creation of an environment in which to live and work is surely one of life's most beautiful experiences. It was in fact a bad time for house-hunting and we had a long and frustrating search, but in the autumn of that year the 'phone rang and we were asked to rush at once to see a house that a widowed lady wished to sell privately. As soon as we sighted the great cedar of Lebanon standing on the front lawn, which seemed to embrace the house, we knew that we had come home. It seemed to me destiny that we should have The Laskett, and it was soon after that we learned the composer Elgar had visited it – that was another sign – my wife had conceived and designed Sir Frederick Ashton's ballet on Elgar's Enigma Variations.

Every time the house figures in what I write the page bursts with joy, even if we are cursing builders or coping with four feet of snow that is engulfing us. I recall that first summer spent there as a kind of golden paradise about which I wrote to my Dutch friend:

'... Our great excitement has been moving to Herefordshire at the beginning of May. This began disastrously with the pantechnicon bearing our beloved objects sailing off the road in a terrible crash with awful consequences for some of our treasures – 22 items smashed to firewood and 50 others badly damaged ... We have settled into Hereford very happily. I feel so much more relaxed ... One sits in the sun and watches the landscape unfolding in every direction or contemplates the great 1812 cedar on the front lawn, or one gardens. I have really become a passionate gardener. Reclamation began with the kitchen garden which is the size of two tennis courts and full of strawberry beds, gooseberries, black-currants. Which area to save and which area to grass over and turn to orchard was the question. We persevere and I reclaim an area each week ... It is glorious picking pound after pound of fruit and deep freezing it or making delicious fresh jams or Julia makes one of her rare appearances in the kitchen to make jellies, pickles and chutneys and other English farmhouse goodies which are bottled and labelled and stored in neat rows in the cupboard. How happy

we are! And the builders? Well, we camp in our rambling house with about three chairs, a trestle table and a bed. Gradually they have taken us over. But it is exciting to see the great breach made in the wall from what will be our hall into our new dining room and watch the whole house gain a new dimension and fill with light and landscape ... Every week we arrive to find progress: windows are carted away, doors are removed and windows replace them, ceilings are taken down, cupboards are inserted and shelves added where we need them. We are months off any organized house but it is bliss ...'

Anything to do with our house has been happy. I turn in my diary to 1979 and there it is again: 'We had the happiest of summers, a break of five weeks through August into September ...' The passage ends, 'It was a blissful break, the longest since 1973 I think and so very much needed. I returned feeling positive, rested, constructive, energetic and refusing to dwell on past woes.'

In this way I articulated onto the page the role that the house and the garden played in sustaining me during a period of public misery. I was embattled. Brought in as the hoped-for reforming Director in 1974, all that I had striven for was dashed to pieces as Government cut the staff by over a hundred in one year, forcing me to shut the museum's service to the regions after over a century and the museum itself one day a week. The personal problems it threw up for the staff were devastating. It was a bloodbath with the unions and my hair turned white. It was at that time that I recorded an encounter with Lady Antonia Fraser. 'She said to me something extraordinary, the drift of which was, now you have private happiness and public misery; before you married you had private anguish and public happiness. How true.'

As the awful late 1970s drew to their close the centrality of marriage, house and garden as embodying a passionate, private, blessed arcadia recurs. 'I hope 1978 will be less horrid than 1976 or 1977' runs the valedictory paragraph to that year, 'There will be a terrific battle . . . but the Unions are against me and they, as you know, run everything (into the ground, I feel like adding) . . . How lucky I am to have Julia and our blissful loving professional existence and this glorious house and garden which I love more than any other patch of earth in the world and which yearly becomes more and more us. Count your blessings.'

And what of the garden? Its story really began in the summer of 1973 when the farmer who rented the field from us for his cattle informed me that he wanted it no longer. Standing looking at the expanse of four foot high grass my wife, noticing that one area was level, said that once there must have been a grass tennis court on part of it, and so we mowed it back and on this terrain planted our first major formal garden. After that furor hortensis set in and the garden now covers four acres with some thirty different 'rooms'. Gardening is an example of new happiness entering life as it unfolds, for I had no interest in gardens until that moment, and from then on it became obsessive. Every time my pen touches the subject the page lights up. Time and again the happiness it has brought me is caught when, for example, in my diary or letters, I wrote about the spring flowers I could glimpse from my writing room window, or the thrill of sitting down in the Rose Garden and finding that the yew hedge I had planted at barely two feet high was now tall enough for me not to be able to see out, let alone the excitement of sculpting it into bastions. 'So we settle in for winter,' I wrote in December 1980, 'The leaves have left the trees. Miss Torte de Shell is on my lap, having scolded me for being a day late. It is a bright sunny day but it is bitterly cold and I look out on the great avenue we call Elizabeth Tudor and long to see the daffodils appear. There is so much to do in the garden.' Or in May 1983: 'Here we have been in a sea of water, rain, rain and more rain. Everything is sodden. There has been only one weekend when the sun shone and then it was gorgeous. It has been, however, the most wonderful spring for flowers, the great avenues were thick with daffodils for over a month and we await the newly planted lime trees, twenty of them, to leaf for the first time. Pray to heaven that they last as that's the third planting so far. Banks are covered with hyacinths and primroses. And the Rembrandt tulips, which I'm crazy about, are beginning to come into bloom in the Rose garden.' And that summer the garden was even more gorgeous: 'This has been the hottest of summers . . . the abundant rain which preceded it has resulted in bloom as never before, roses above all in abundance, the branches so heavy with flowers that they bend to the earth. In the garden the picture composes after a decade, and the main worry is the mileage of hedge trimming and pruning to sustain the effect. I go to the far side of the 'field' and cut the yew into a box and wire the leaders to form peacocks. The arbour and seat opposite are then clipped and cut back. They stand now virtually complete, but somehow my mind was full of how to tidy it up, how to cope with one's mistakes and how to give it all a bit more finish.'

In 1992 the editor of the garden magazine *Hortus* asked me to write about our garden, what inspired it and how it was made. It was conceived in a dark hour, 1974, the year of the three day week, the coal miners' strike, roaring inflation and the threat of a wealth tax, planted in defiance of this threat to a great English tradition, the making of a country house garden. I never cease to give thanks that I have lived to see that vulnerable vision fulfilled, something which I could not have guessed would happen at its inception. In the final paragraph of that article I summed up what the garden means to me:

'If you asked what The Laskett garden was about, I might reply that it is the portrait of a marriage, the family we never had (or wanted), a unique mnemonic landscape peopled with the ghosts of nearly everyone we have loved, both living and dead. It has always been conceived as an enclosed private world, and that indeed is the key. There is no borrowed landscape. It deliberately shuts out the glory of the rolling hills of Herefordshire and remains a sealed, hermetic, magical domain of its own. And yet there is never a sense of being shut in, of claustrophobia. Just one of serene tranquillity, or as much of it as can be granted in this transitory life. For me its making has been more extraordinary than any of the books I have written or museums I have directed. To take a basket with a bottle of wine and two glasses up to the Victoria & Albert Museum Temple on a summer's evening, and sit contemplating the vista together in silence, is happiness quantified. Can anyone ask for more?'

As I get older gardens cast an ever more potent spell over me. If I walk into a marvellous garden I am enraptured. My spirits soar. All my intellect and senses swirl in a mad rush as though to paradise. The sense of excitement, of drama, of heightened perception is almost tangible to me. Rain, leaden skies, howling gales, nothing can impede the acute awareness of being engaged with a miracle in which art has tamed nature. I am as happy seeing a garden in winter as in the fullness of summer. It makes absolutely no difference. Every season, every play of light brings its own sense of beauty. Each spring still remains a revelation ... I write this having just strolled through the garden on a cold late autumn day when it has been shot with sudden shafts of sunlight. Everywhere I looked there was joy. Along the pleached lime avenue we call Elizabeth Tudor the swagged beech hedge linking the limes is an incredible tapestry of ochres, browns and yellows with lingering flecks of the summer's green. Above it flutter the as yet unfallen lime leaves like golden medallions, the fallen ones luminous on the grass avenue beneath. In the garden we planted to mark the Queen's Silver Jubilee there is that last flush of roses, scattered touches of white in the manner of a pointilliste painting giving sparkle to a garden otherwise already laid to rest for the winter. But even where that has happened there is joy to be had, for this is the time of year when the garden's structure takes over, giving the onlooker the aesthetic of architecture. In my stroll I passed the flower garden, one half of which I'd just put to bed, and reflected on

THE
JUBILEE
GARDEN
1977

how handsome the bold topiary shapes of yew and golden holly look on such a morning, for in summer they lose their identity amidst a profusion of bloom. And everywhere such colour: the quince trees weighed down with their fruit glowing like golden lanterns, the deep purple of the berberis hedges dappled with scarlet berries, the incredible incandescent colour of the medlar trees like flaming torches, the bright orange of the hips still on some of the specie roses and the malus spangled with fruits in buttery yellows and shades of puce. Could there be greater happiness than such a walk just outside one's garden door?

But, have I never had happiness in my public life, then? Turning the pages of those diaries and letters I really began to wonder. But one thing did catch my eye. On 27 December 1969 I wrote a review of the year to my Dutch friend. It had been a fantastic one, almost an apotheosis, and its climax had been an exhibition, *The Elizabethan Image*, which I staged at the Tate Gallery. This I conceived as a great spectacle of sunshine and shade treated in an unashamedly theatrical manner but aimed at achieving one thing, to make a public which had never looked at Elizabethan and Jacobean painting leave the exhibition as though they had undergone some revelatory experience. I am immodest enough to say that I achieved my object. They queued to get in . What I wrote was revealing and a testament as to how I saw one part of my role as a museum director:

'*The Elizabethan Image* is undoubtedly the best exhibition I have ever done. And scholastically? Well, it made its point. But the great thing was to give a great section of the public a happy and joyous hour and a half. I have never before been quite so overcome over this aspect – it has come back to me again and again from various people . . .'

So this sudden realization brings another expression of happiness into my life and a far less selfish one; the ability to give it. I have always been acutely aware of attempting to give people delight, of not letting institutions which I have directed become ego trips for the curators. There is nothing wrong with sweeping people away into bliss, particularly during dark periods when the public needs something to lift flagging spirits (a role occupied also by theatre.) That is not to downgrade their obverse side, their ability to provoke and disturb. That aim of purveying unalloyed delight, escapism if you will, brings to mind a letter of Ellen Terry's, to Bernard Shaw. He was always goading her to appear in the new drama of Ibsen instead of wasting her time, as he saw it, acting as prop to Henry Irving in his Shakespeare productions. Ellen Terry didn't see it like that. What was wrong, she asked, in giving tired working people two hours of happiness through her ability to waft them for a short period of time to another world, one in which she would dance and sing and the stage would be filled with fairies and other marvels.

I had become conscious of the possibility of giving people happiness at an even earlier date, before *The Elizabethan Image*. I recall vividly the exact moment when that discovery was made. I was a post-graduate student under the formidable Renaissance scholar Dame Frances Yates, writing a thesis on Elizabethan court pageantry and at that period I was immensely shy and introspective, dedicated to the obscurer byways of the world of learning but, through her, I was asked to give a lecture which was part of an extension course at the Victoria & Albert Museum. This was the first time that I had ever performed in public – if the scattering of some sixty to a hundred people gathered to hear an unknown young man may be categorized as such. The lecture was on 'Pageantry in the Elizabethan Court Year.' I felt safe, as it was illustrated with slides and as soon as I began the house lights went out, so that I was unaware of the audience, which calmed my nerves. I spoke with all the passion of youth. At the end, when the lights came on again, two old people came up to me, they said 'Oh, thank you, thank you, we did enjoy that.' It was the first time that I was conscious of giving information and pleasure to other people, just through communicating one's own knowledge. It had an indelible effect. How wonderful, I thought. It had never occurred to me that being a scholar could bring with it the ability to give joy to the wider world.

Indeed, that lecture contributed to my carving out a life dedicated to holding the middle ground. Up until then I had been led along a path in which scholarship was held to be a sacred trust but also one only for the chosen, its fruits to be communicated at best to the illuminati. I revolted against that and I have never minded the charge of populism. It was an attitude that helped colour the success of my National Portrait Gallery years. I never hesitated to break the rules in the interest of the visitor. Some of the most successful exhibitions, the one of Cecil Beaton's photographs or the parade of beauties through the centuries, attracted the wrath of the die-hards and thunderbolts from *The Burlington Magazine*. Who cares? The public adored them.

At the Victoria & Albert Museum I often encapsulated my aim for the institution in a phrase from Sir Philip Sidney's *Arcadia*. He is describing a tournament, at which knights appeared in esoteric disguises, and he wrote that they embodied 'the riches of knowledge upon the stream of delight.' Whether delight counts as happiness I'm not sure, but to engender in the visitor wonder and pleasure as a preliminary to knowledge is not a bad aim for a museum director. How much happiness the V & A gave to the public during the fourteen years I directed it I do not know. I was aware that I was attempting to do that, at least in one aspect but inevitably, a director's desk is the receiving house for complaints rather than eulogies. Yet I cannot think but that those who came to the great Renaissance jewellery exhibition, say, or that on the history of British gardens, were not given an hour or two's happy enchantment.

Writing is another matter. If academic writing can hardly aspire to purvey happiness, I have realized since I left those pastures that other forms of writing clearly do. For seven years I contributed periodically to a column in the magazine *Country Life* called Country Week. In it I described the life we lead in Herefordshire, the passage of the seasons, what was happening in the garden, the house with its manifold activities, from marmalade-making to taking the cat for a walk. That, I know, had a huge following; readers who would write to me about this or that, or sometimes I had an encounter with one of them, like the time outside the Alhambra in Cordoba, when someone wandered up to me and asked about our cat Muff. Occasionally, out of the blue, someone will pluck up courage to say 'Thank you for all the pleasure you've given me,' as once when I was at Paddington Station queuing to get a ticket. A woman suddenly recognized me, hesitated and then said, 'Oh, I'm sure you hate being recognized and bothered by people.' 'No' I replied, 'far from it. It's a very lonely life as a writer, hunched over a computer screen all day and never knowing whether anyone out there likes what you're doing or not.' And then she shyly thanked me for everything I had given her through my work. 'Oh, I'll write to you about it !' She saw me hesitate at that point as through my mind flashed the thought of yet another letter to reply to. And then she said, 'I'll make it a postcard!' and I beamed with pleasure. For me it was a touching and treasured encounter, for what more can any creative person ask than to contribute even in a small way to someone else's happiness?

I should ask whether works of art have given me happiness, for I have spent most of my life writing about them, looking at them, handling them – and raising money to buy them. The answer must be 'yes', and the 'yes' is reinforced by that list of things which one wishes to return to again and again. Mine could be a long one; any selection has to be arbitrary. Golden Vermeer comes pretty high, supremely his View of Delft in the Mauritshuis, the panorama across from the quayside with its scattered figures towards the town reflected in the waters, its roofs caught in a shaft of sunlight. I always sit and stare at that, overwhelmed by its economy and the sheer tranquillity of mood it exudes. The great Hugo van der Goes altarpiece of the Portanari family in the Uffizi draws me, even if only to contemplate the blue

HUGO
VAN
DER
GOES
920

and white maiolica vase with its sprays of lilies and aquilegias placed in the foreground, and then the frescoes by Giotto in the Arena Chapel in Padua. Was ever the Bible story told with more drama, tenderness and compassion? I doubt it, for they impose by their power silent contemplation. So does the astounding Van Eyck altarpiece in Ghent, which reduces even the most vociferous to a muted whisper. One moves around it as though in the presence of the supernatural. Almost any late Titian fills me with wonder, just the touch, or rather smear of the paint onto the canvas is so miraculous that I am left in awe, happy to share, five centuries on, the summation of genius.

And Veronese's frescoes in the Palladio's Villa Barbaro at Maser. I think I would choose that building, for it embodied the last flickering optimism of renaissance civilization before it was dashed by the religious dissension and intolerance which was to

cast a sombre shadow over Europe for the next two hundred years. Here in one building I see gathered all that is best and happiest in Western European civilization at one of its apogees. I feel held by the proportion of the building, for it was built as an earthly reflection of the harmony of heaven; and then those frescoes, celebrating all that was greatest and most joyous about renaissance culture, the rediscovery of nature caught in vistas of verdant, arcadian landscape through painted columns, or the festoons of grapes on rustic pergolas which straddle the ceiling. Here the virtues reign, here the weapons of war, lances, swords and staves are put to one side and one's eyes are directed upwards to those who make music in such a way that one can almost hear it. Here is the happiness and optimism of another age projected through time for those who wish to look and understand. There are endearing small touches of enchantment – a little girl peeping through a door, a spaniel looking inquisitive and a tortoiseshell cat playing tea cosy. This is high art and humanity. For me it is always a radiant experience. Enough . . . This is a list as long or as short as the proverbial piece of string, and I could go on, to embrace those moments in life lightened by great poetry and prose, opera, ballet and theatre, and then on again to encounters with the natural world which have left their mark as happy experiences.

But they also embody something else which is less concerned with happiness than with the human spirit. Everything so far has cast me into being a child of the Enlightenment and of my own time, to those ages when the pursuit of happiness in this life became an exciting possibility. How could I be otherwise? Each and every form of happiness I have so far discussed belongs firmly to the voyage of life as expressed through the intellect, the imagination and the emotions. But there is a part of me which embraces firmly happiness as it was seen by the pre-Enlightenment world, as something in a sense not attainable in the present. This attitude is caught by Sir Thomas Browne in his *Religio Medici*: 'Certainly there is no happiness within this circle of flesh, nor is it in the optics of these eyes to behold felicity; the first day of our Jubilee is death.' What Browne has in mind is something quite different from anything I have touched upon until now. He is concerned with man's inner journey which, in the late twentieth century, may take many forms – and often none at all. That I make that journey as a Catholic Anglican is my own choice, but it has seen me through. It has also given me the devotional milieu to which I most respond, the world of George Herbert, Henry Vaughan and Thomas Traherne. Indeed, it is the latter who provides me with the peroration I need for this celebration of happiness, for it lifts it onto another level – that of the mystic visionary.

When we came to live in Herefordshire I had not made the connection with Thomas Traherne. He was the son of a Hereford shoemaker and, although he ended up as chaplain to Sir Orlando Bridgeman at Teddington in Middlesex, he was rector for a time in the 1660s of Credenhill, not far from us. His most famous work, the *Centuries of Meditations* was, it is generally accepted, written for a Herefordshire woman. What made him write it is summed up in one sentence. 'There was never a tutor that did professly teach Felicity, though that be the mistress of all other sciences.' And his mystical poetry and prose sing of that quest in a way I find deeply appealing to the late twentieth century mind. Traherne wrote as follows.

'Felicity is a thing coveted of all. The whole world is taken with the beauty of it: and he is no man, but a stock or stone that does not desire it. Nevertheless great offence hath been done by the philosphers and scandal given, through their blindness, many of them, in making Felicity to consist in negatives. They tell us it doth not consist in riches, it doth not consist in honours, it doth not consist in pleasures. Wherein, saith a miserable man, doth it consist? Why in contentment, in self sufficiency, in virtues, in the right government of our passions, and etc. Were it not better to show the amiableness of virtues, and the benefits of the right government of our passions, the objects of contentment, and the grounds of self sufficiency, by the truest means? Which these never do. Ought they not to distinguish between true and false riches as our Saviour doth; between real and feigned honours; between clear and pure pleasures and those which are muddy and unwholesome? . . . The amiableness of virtue consisteth in this, that by it all happiness is either attained or enjoyed. Contentment and rest ariseth from a full perception of infinite treasures. So that whosoever will profit in the mystery of Felicity, must see the objects of his happiness, and the manner how they are to be enjoyed, and discern also the powers of his soul by which he is to enjoy them, and perhaps the rules that shall guide him in the way of enjoyment. All which things you have here, GOD, THE WORLD, YOURSELF. ALL THINGS in Time and Eternity being the objects of your Felicity, God the Giver, you the receiver.'

What gives me happiness may not give happiness to someone else. For me it is a strange web of things which criss-cross each other; friendship, living each day as though it were one's last, never going back but only forward, looking for the good things in everyone, the passage of the seasons in a landscape or a garden, cooking a good meal and sharing it, being together with the person you love most, trying never to nurse past resentments, filling one's environment with a clutter of things which are the repository of felicitous memory, expecting nothing as a rule of life, so that anything which comes is an unlooked-for blessing, and above all, attempting, as a priest once bade me, to make each day a perpetual awareness of the presence of God. And although I may have inherited a disposition to happiness, what strikes me most is that in spite of it every one of these things has to be worked at, which gives some substance to the evidence that happiness does involve the exercise of choice. The maxims of my life only fell into place by my half century. I would have been far happier if I had reached some of them earlier; but that is the marvel of age, each decade bringing forth its own fruits.

I am also struck forcibly by how unhappiness has its place in this scheme of things, for through experiencing it we formulate what for us constitutes its opposites – contentment, joy, happiness; and that discovery, which only comes with the passing of time, not only affects our choices in life but makes us guard as sacred those things which make up the pantheon wherein resides our bliss. Life, one must recognize, is transitory, and, I have sometimes thought, that if there is to be any sort of gathering after my death, – which I naturally hope is still a good way off – it will be of the kind Dame Sybil Thorndike once described, in a reminiscence which she performed at the National Portrait Gallery, of the actress Ellen Terry. She ended what I shall always treasure as a memorable and moving performance, by quoting from a letter written by someone who had been at the great actress's funeral. The sentence has stuck in my mind.

'It was all flowers and happiness and Edward Gordon Craig was heard to remark, "We must have more days like this . . ."'

HERZOG
FREDERICK
VON SANS
SOUCI